J.

DEDICATION

This Book is dedicated to all who desire the utmost from their relationships. Because you deserve nothing less than extraordinary.

J.

Relationship Breakthrough

Achieve Massive Success In Your Relationship That Others Would Kill For

J. S. PARKER

Copyright © 2016 J. S. PARKER

All rights reserved.

CONTENTS

RELATIONSHIP BREAKTHROUGH

1	Book 1 Introduction	1
2	Chapter 1: Why Do You Need These Secret Keys for A Relationship Breakthrough?	2
3	Chapter 2: Secret Key 1 - Desire	5
4	Chapter 3: Secret Key 2 - Feeling of Security	23
5	Chapter 4: Secret Key 3 - Respect and Compassion	29
6	Chapter 5: Secret Key 4 - Confidence	41
7	Chapter 6: Secret Key 5 – Give and Take the Lead	50
8	Book 2 Introduction	54
9	Chapter 1: What Do You Want?	56
10	Chapter 2: Secret Key 1 – Open, Honest, Consistent Communication	61
11	Chapter 3: Secret Key 2 – Equality and Respect	73
12	Chapter 4: Secret Key 3 – Acceptance for Who They Are	80
13	Chapter 5: Secret Key 4 – The Pedestal	87
14	Chapter 6: Secret Key 5 – Make Her Smile	91
15	Chapter 7: Special Bonus Tips	94

15

16 Conclusion   107

J.

J.

ACKNOWLEDGEMENTS

INTRODUCTION

Hello there, and thank you for purchasing this book. For women: In the pages you are about to read for the first book, you will discover the keys that would help you achieve a relationship breakthrough with your man. For Men: You will discover what women are actually looking for in their relationship with you. Do understand and grasp every detail provided. In the following book 2 also included in this set, this process will be reversed. You will then learn the flip side of the coin to attain a holistic view of what it takes for a successful relationship with others. Whether you are in a marriage, dating or even single, these keys will help you on your journey to being in the most blissful relationship possible. I hope you enjoy this book, and find it informational.

CHAPTER 1

WHAT ARE THESE SECRET KEYS TO A RELATIONSHIP BREAKTHROUGH?

Have you ever wondered why so many people fail in their relationship with men, whether as friends or more than that? Wondered why so many couples break up, even though it seemed like they would be together forever? Do you have a hard time connecting with men enough to take your relationship to the highest level possible? Many people do, and that is because they do not know about these secret keys for a breakthrough.

It is essential to know what men want and need, otherwise, you will not be able to know him as well as you wish you could, and the distance will make it hard to connect. A connection is important when in a relationship, as it is what determines the amount of passion you have years down the road. A weak connection makes for weak passion and limited intimacy once the honeymoon phase is over.

If you do not have passion and intimacy in a marriage, this can be a major problem, as they are what keep the love alive, and the marriage interesting. Without any interest in your marriage, it can cause many problems, including divorce, and infidelity.

So to avoid these issues you must learn about the secret keys, for without them you will be destined to have an average relationship, rather than a superb relationship. Which an average one can last forever, but a superb relationship will most definitely last forever.

Only about twenty percent of people know about these keys to a man's heart. They are the couples that you see that are eighty years old and still acting like young lovers. They are the couples that everyone aspires to be. These people are the happiest couples alive because they learned the secret keys to marriage, and to unlock their man's heart.

Why it is Pertinent to Know these Keys

These keys are the basis of obtaining a strong and intimate relationship. Almost everyone's goal in life is to get married, and have that marriage last forever. They want to be the couple that everyone looks up to, and that everyone comes to for advice.

That is where these keys come in. They are designed to help you achieve that level of a relationship in your life. These are from a man's perspective, to help you understand more what they really want. Not what women say they want.

A man's heart is unique. It is unlike a woman's heart in many ways, and should be treated as such. You should want to know exactly how to open his heart to show you exactly how he wants to be loved.

Men are also stubborn at times. You may have already won his heart, but he has put up walls to try to prevent himself from falling. You have to break through these walls as well, which if you use these keys, should be easier than just whacking away at it with charm. Read on to find these keys.

Chapter 2:

Secret Key #1

Desire

Men do not say this aloud, which is why this key is such a big secret, but men love romance. They want their partners to put in a little romantic effort as well. This key is important, as without it, a man cannot be sure if you are really down for him or not. If he doesn't feel like you desire him, he will not completely open up to you. Very few couples realize how important this is, and that is why often times, you see relationships fizzle out so fast. Follow this key to strengthen your bond with the male species.

Romance

Describe your most romantic fantasy. Is it elaborate? Or simple? Either way, you most likely still have one. So does he. Men are romantic creatures by nature, but they also like to be romanced. Take him out to dinner, and pick up the check. Take him out to the movies, and pay for him. Return the favor he probably often shows you quite frequently.

It doesn't even have to be that expensive either. When he has a long day at work, surprise him with his favorite dinner served by candlelight. In his day off, pack a picnic lunch, and drive to his favorite spot and enjoy a picnic. It doesn't have to always be fancy, you just need to put in as much effort into showing him you want him, as he does for you.

It is about feeling wanted, and loved. If you aren't putting in an effort to show him how much you care, how is he going to know that you are going to be there in the long run? He will feel like you are only there for what he can do for you, not what you can do together, and he will begin to feel used. Value a man. Don't expect to get treated like royalty if you are only going to treat him like a peasant.

To understand more about being romantic for a guy, this scenario will help you to understand more, that it isn't always about the big things, sometimes even the smallest gesture means the world to a guy.

Scenario

James looked over at his girlfriend, and wondered if she truly loved him. She said it all the time, but how did he know for sure? Was she just fronting to get his money or was she truly his ride or die chick? How could he be sure that she really loved him?

"Babe?" He called over to MaryBeth

"Yes, baby?" She replied

"Answer three questions for me. What is my favorite color? What was my favorite memory as a child? What is my favorite food?" James needed to know if she loved him as much as he loved her. He knew that her favorite color was purple, because it reminded her of the twilight hours when everything is quiet and still. He knew that her favorite childhood memory was when her dad took some free bikes and pieced them together to make her very first bike because they were too poor to buy a new one. He knew that her favorite food was Italian, and that it only became so when she met him, because he was Italian, and showed her how real cuisine was created, rather than restaurants that order frozen food and heat it up in a microwave. He wanted to see if she knew the answers to those questions.

"You don't have a favorite color, per say. You are color blind. You say that your favorite color would be emerald green because that is the color I told you my eyes were. Your favorite childhood memory was when you and your brother climbed the big oak tree in your backyard together, and talked about life and what your plans were for your futures. You said that was the first time you two had really ever bonded, and that was when you realized you wanted to be a real estate investor. You were nine. Your favorite food is Chinese, because it reminds you of when your mother used to take you to a Chinese restaurant every Friday for mother-son bonding time. The last time you did that with her was two days before she died. You used to dislike Chinese food, but went because she loved it, but after she died, the memories made you love it." She answered. "Now tell me. What is this about?"

"I was wondering if you loved me. No girl has ever paid enough attention to me, and focused mainly on my wallet. You answered every question perfectly. The first one to ever do so. I love you so much."

"How could you doubt I love you, James? I may not have a lot of money, but I try to show you every day that I love you. You should think about that, rather than focusing on little questions that anyone who pays attention to you could answer." MaryBeth replied, slightly offended that he felt she didn't love him.

As she walked out of the room, James sat and thought about what she said. He thought back over the course of their relationship, and thought about all the things she did for him regularly.

She cooks me dinner on a regular basis. When I have had a hard day, she rubs my back. Even though she is on her feet for over eight hours a day, and mine is just stress of a tenant not wanting to pay rent. She shows up on my longer days with my favorite meal, and we eat it together before we have to go back to work. For no reason at all, she told me to get in the car, and we drove to our favorite spot with some fast food, and ate while watching the trains pull into the station.

She always tells me she loves me before she goes to bed, even if she is angry with me. She never fails to ask me how my day was, and truly listen to the answer. Even though sometimes I tune her out when she talks about hers. I don't know what her favorite song is, or when her first heartbreak happened, but she sure as hell know mine. What have I done for her? I know the answer to three questions that anyone with half a brain could answer, and I buy her stuff. I take her out to fancy dinners, and spend money on her but that is about it, and yet she never questions my love for her. I want to marry this woman. She is my everything. She has a piece of me that no one else ever will. She truly has my heart.

James walked back into the bedroom, where he found MaryBeth crying. He sat beside her, and began to rub her back.

"I'm sorry. I am so sorry I ever doubted your love for me. I know I could say that every other girlfriend has only wanted my money, and it broke me, but in truth; I am just an ass. I love you, MaryBeth. I want to marry you someday. Not today, we still have a lot of things to work through, but if you forgive me, I promise that one day you will have an engagement ring on your finger." James said, pulling out a little ring and sliding it on her ring finger. "Do you accept my promise?"

"Yes. I forgive you as well." MaryBeth said, beaming with happiness while her eyes were still brimming with tears.

Discussion

James didn't realize until it was brought to his attention, all the little things that MaryBeth does for him to show her love. Sometimes you do have to give him a little wake up call to show him that you do play the romance card on a regular basis. Maybe do a big gesture here and there to really show him you care. But sometimes it just takes you telling him to think that gets his brain in gear. Be romantic, and even if he doesn't realize it at first, he will start to see all the little things you do for him, even when he doesn't notice you doing them.

Desire

You have to ignite a white-hot passion in him that makes him want to take you right here and right now almost any where you go. This desire is what fuels the passion in your relationship. If there is no passion, things get stale, and that is when people drift apart the most. If the bedroom isn't rocking, you better get packing, because you need a good sex life, and desire filled relationship to last for a long time.

How do you ignite this desire in him? It is simple. You have to desire him as well. Men are easily enticed, if you are willing to tap into your animalistic nature. You have to want to make him desire you, so that means you will have to be pro-active in your sexuality, and prove your prowess in the bedroom, along with outside the bedroom.

How is this done exactly? Ditch the missionary position. This is the bane of all sexual existence. There are so many more positions out there, where you don't have to lie there like a lifeless doll and take what he is giving you. (Ditch standard doggy style for gay couples. This is the missionary in the gay world.) Look up new positions and try them for yourselves. Try different styles. There are some that can spice up the bedroom if you are both willing to try it.

- BDSM: This is a type of sexual style that requires one partner to be dominant, and one partner to be submissive. Start out slow. Don't go "Fifty Shades of Grey" level the first day. Ease into it. Find out the limitations your bodies can handle, how tight you like the collars and ties, what you absolutely do not like, and so on and so forth. Knowing what you like is important, as if you don't like it, the experience will not be fun. Both of you have to be vocal if you want to know what each other likes and don't like. Also, come up with a safe word to use, so in the heat of the moment, you don't hurt yourselves.

- Roleplay: This is one for when you want to experience what it is like to have sex with someone different, yet still wanting that sex to be with your partner. You get little costumes, and you dress up as someone else. While dressed up as another person, you literally become that person. You are not yourself, you are a whole other person. This could mean you have your guy become the cable guy, or you become his secretary. There are many other people you can take on the role of, such as famous people, or make up your own personas. If you do not feel comfortable with role play, but are still intrigued by it, try it on a small scale. Have him be a fake person you make up, and vice versa. This will get you more comfortable with the idea, so you can more enjoy it.

- Making a Home Video: This can be a very good bonding experience in the bedroom, as you can watch back the video you make, and see how much you were enjoying the sex. Once you both realize how good things are in the bedroom, you will never want to leave. Relax and enjoy it, though. Don't try to put on a show just because you are being filmed. You aren't a porn star, and neither is he. Just enjoy it. You can also see what positions work for you, and what doesn't when you play the video back. These videos should never be put on the internet, or used for any other reason than your viewing pleasure. If handled correctly, they can make for great material to get you in the mood as well.

- Watch Porn Together: This can give you an idea on positions to try, and also get you in the mood to do the deed. Find a video that you both like, and settle in. You can also try a bit of self stimulation while watching the video, but be careful not to distract yourself, or your partner from the video itself. The whole point is to learn new positions and bond. Remember though, porn is an act. Do not expect to have super explosive orgasms the first time you try a position. You most likely will have to practice a few times for it to even feel good.

There are many ways to spark up some interest in the bedroom, but how do you make him want to do these things? How do you spark the carnal desire in him? How do you show him you want him so bad it makes your stomach do flips? There are a few ways that are fool proof.

- Send Him Little Notes: You can leave sticky notes all over the house for him, in his car, in his lunchbox if he has one. You can also text him all the things you would like to do to him.

Tell him that you aren't wearing any underwear or something like that. Give him something to want later that night.

- Tease Him: Kiss him seductively in the hall way and then keep moving along. Rub your rear against his junk, and then walk away. Play footsie with him when you eat dinner. Make him desire you, turn him on, but then leave him hanging. At the end of the night he will want you so bad, he will do anything to have you.

- Be Playful: Sometimes the biggest turn on is when you act like a kid. Being free-spirited can be the biggest turn on for guys, because they like knowing you are happy and having fun. Tickle him, and then make him chase you to the bedroom and tackle you on the bed. Play wrestle a little bit, and watch the playing turn into sex real fast. Sometimes the best foreplay, is to simply play.

You have to create a white-hot desire in the pit of his stomach, one that makes him crave you when you are away, and not want to leave your side when you are near. You have to make him think about you constantly, to the point where he doesn't even want you to go to the restroom because that means being away from you for too long.

This desire will unlock the part of his heart that makes him want to commit. He won't want to leave, because he is too devoted to you, and he loves you way too much to walk away from everything you have together. You have to keep this desire alive, and strong, to keep the relationship strong and healthy.

Here is a scenario that should help you get a mental picture of what that desire looks like. Caution. This one is mildly graphic, but if you are an adult reading this, as the disclaimer warns, you have probably read much worse.

Scenario

He wanted her. He wanted her more than he has ever wanted anyone. The way she teased him drove him insane. It was like she took pleasure in keeping him aroused to the point of pain. She would pay for it, when she finally let him have her. These thoughts swirled around Mason's brain, and left him winded. He thought back to when they first met.

Lacy wasn't like a lot of girls. That is what attracted Mason to her. He was tired of girls throwing themselves at him. He was tired of girls who had nothing more to offer than a loose vagina, and some amateur head. These women bored Mason, so he never kept them around much longer than a night. Lacy, however, showed very little interest in Mason when they first met. She looked him up and down, offered her hand in a professional manner, and said it was nice to meet him. Like she was at a job interview. She didn't blush, or swoon, or make any indication that she found Mason attractive. He had to have her. She was exactly what he wanted. A challenging woman.

He became more and more infatuated with her as the night drew on, and he listened to her talk, and engaged in conversation with her. She was Harvard educated, and it showed. She wasn't haughty or anything, really she was very humble, but when she spoke her words were eloquent and well thought out. She didn't use 'like' in between every word, as most girls tend to do. Instead, every word out of her mouth was carefully planted like she was speaking a puzzle.

She turned him on. Plain, and simple. He had to have a date with her.

"Excuse me, Lacy? I am enamored by your eloquence, and would love to talk to you more, one-on-one. Would you care to have a cup of coffee with me after this party is over?" Mason asked

"Why don't we leave right now? I feel I am boring everyone else." Lacy said

"I highly doubt you are boring anyone, but if you wish, I would love to go at once."

They left the club, and walked down the street to a little coffee shop that was open twenty four hours a day. This was one of Mason's spots to think, and he wanted Lacy to experience it as well. When they walked in, he could tell that she was star-struck with the place. It wasn't well known, but it was cozy. He offered to buy her coffee, but she refused, stating that she was glad to have an excuse to leave the club.

"I hope you don't think that I am like other girls, Mason." Lacy said as soon as the found a cozy nook to sit down.

"I beg you are pardon?" Mason nearly choked on his latte

"I don't put out on the first date. You have to win my heart. You can't just bring me to a quaint little coffee shop, and expect me to sleep with you tonight." Lacy was blunt with what she spoke, there was no beating around the bush.

"Of course I don't think you are like other girls. In fact, I have never brought a woman here before."

As if on cue, the shop owner came out then to greet Mason.

"Mason, my old friend. Are you enjoying your evening? Oh! You have a lady with you! Forgive me for interrupting, I have never seen this before. Enjoy yourselves." The shop owner ducked back into his office with a bright red face.

"Well I guess I don't need to ask you to prove that you have never brought a woman here."

They sat and talked the night away. In the wee hours of the morning, Mason drove Lacy home, as her friends had already left the club.

"Lacy, can I see you again?" Mason asked, as she stepped out of the car.

"I would like that very much."

Three months later, Lacy practically lived with him. They often slept in the same bed. And he still had not been able to make love to her. That is what he wanted. He didn't want to just have sex with her, he wanted to make love to her.

"What is on your mind, Mace?" Lacy asked, sitting on his lap.

"I want you, Lacy. More than I have ever wanted anyone. I love you. I truly love you. I want to make passionate love to you, in a way no man ever has. I want to give you the world, if you will let me. You are the one I want. Forever."

"Mason, that is what I have been wanting to hear since we met. Tonight you will finally get what you want. Me."

That night was the most mind blowing night of Mason's life. Lacy felt perfect for him. They didn't leave the bedroom for hours. Everything was perfect.

Flash forward two years later, and Lacy still teased him. He still wanted her as much as he did from day one. He couldn't imagine life with any other woman, as she was the only one who lit such a desire in him.

Discussion

Lacy made Mason desire her, by not always being readily available. She let him know she was into him, but she did not give up everything from the beginning, and even after she gave it all up, she still kept that playfulness up in the relationship, making him want her bad enough to always desire her.

This is what you have to do in a relationship. You have to keep your partner interested in you. Don't think that just because you have been together for a long time, that means you have to act like an old couple. Be playful. Show each other how much you care.

Chapter 3: Secret Key #2

Make Him Feel Safe

Men will never admit that they need to feel safe in a relationship. This key is a secret, because society makes men feel that they have to be macho all the time. This is the furthest from the truth, and you should not believe this, as everyone needs to feel safe. Not just physically, but emotionally.

Couples that know this often have less fights, and less time spent angry at each other. Fights and arguments do not stem from someone doing something that you don't agree with, they stem from being afraid that they are going to leave you. You get angry because you don't feel safe, and you are scared you are going to be left alone, so you throw up a wall. Men do the same thing as everyone else. Only they will never admit that is why they have a wall up.

You have to make him want to take all of his walls down and be open with you. Make him feel like you want to know everything about him. Not just where he grew up, what his favorite color is, and what music does he like. Ask him if he ever sucked his thumb, did he have a teddy bear or a blankie? What was his favorite television show growing up? Has he ever been in trouble? What are his aspirations, and fears? Ask him about his nightmares. Do not be satisfied with one word answers. Give him information about you every time he divulges something about himself.

Emotional Safety

You have to be his safety net as he is free-falling into love with you, just as he has to be yours. You have to catch each other, and you can't fall if you don't trust the other person with your heart. Be open always. You can't expect him to open up to you when you won't open up to him. It is a give and take relationship, when you want to unlock the part of his heart he holds dearest to him.

To make him feel emotionally safe, you have to let him know that you won't let him down. This often means listening to him talk about things you aren't necessarily interested in.

A man has to be able to cry around you to feel truly and completely safe in a relationship. Sometimes you have to assure him that it is okay to cry. Hold him when you see him having a weak moment, and let him know that sometimes even the strongest mountain breaks down. If he can't cry around you, he won't be truly open to you. Men are at their most vulnerable moments in life when they break down in front of someone, because they are bred to believe that crying means you are weak. So if a man finally cries in front of you, you have won his heart.

Here is a scenario of how to know if you make him feel emotionally safe.

Scenario

Josh loved his boyfriend very much, but he felt as if Alex was still closed off. Josh was definitely the more feminine of the two, so he was very open with Alex. Alex however, often changed the subject when it came to his past. Josh knew that Alex loved him, he just wasn't ready to completely open up. Josh was understanding, and never pushed, but still let his love know that he was there for him.

One day, Alex came home in a horrible mood. Josh didn't know what was wrong, but he ran up and hugged Alex anyway.

"Oh, baby, I can just tell you had a horrible day. Would you like to talk about it?" Josh asked.

"Actually I would like that very much, babe." Alex said with a tight throat.

"Come sit down darling, let me make you your favorite tea while you compose your thoughts."

Josh hurried off to the kitchen, while Alex sat down on the couch, looking lost and forlorn. Josh's hear broke just looking at how sad his love looked. After the tea finished brewing, Josh hurried back into the living room, and handed Alex his tea, made just the way he liked it.

"What happened love?" Josh asked gently.

"I guess there is no sense in beating around the bush. My brother is dead. He was shot in the head last night in a drug deal gone wrong." Alex said

"I am so sorry love. I didn't know you had a brother, but I am heartbroken for you nonetheless." Josh said, wrapping his arms around Alex.

"I didn't talk about him much because I was ashamed of him. He was a drug addict. He was always asking when he could meet you, and I always made excuses. I feel horrible now, because he was the only one who supported me when I came out as gay. My parents kicked me out, and he gave me a place to stay. He was the only family I had, and I judged him for something he had about as much control over as I do being gay." Alex broke down in tears.

Josh sat there and held Alex, his heart breaking for him, as it also beamed with love, because Alex was finally opening up to him. He was sad that Alex's only true family was dead, but happy that Alex trusted him enough to tell him everything. His heart swelled with love for the man in his arms crying his eyes out.

Discussion

Alex was very closed off when it came to talking about his past, because it hurt to much to talk about, and he didn't want to cry in front of Josh, and Josh felt distanced from Alex due to his wall he threw up. Once Alex finally started talking about himself, Josh knew that Alex truly loved him, and that he trusted him finally. This gave Josh a happy feeling, even in the midst of a sad time, which allowed him to truly comfort Alex in his moment of need.

Why Do You Need This Key Again?

This key is essential in opening up an intense bond between you and your partner. When you feel comfortable enough to be completely open with each other, you learn more about the other than you could ever imagine. This is important, because to truly love someone, you have to truly know them. Once you truly know everything about someone, loving them becomes a whole lot easier.

Chapter 4:

Secret Key #3

Respect and Compassion

What is the one thing that anyone wants more than anything in the world? That is right, respect. Respect is rated the number one thing that a person wants in life. It is even more of a priority than love, because you can't have love if you don't have respect.

Respect is what makes the world go round. Think Aretha Franklin. R-E-S-P-E-C-T. This song is about how just a little respect can make a world of difference. You have to respect your partner not only as your partner, but as a human being as well. You can't expect them to be perfect, and you have to respect that sometimes they have to make mistakes.

This is where compassion comes in. When your partner makes a mistake, it is always important to show them compassion and understanding. This way they know that you care enough to help them make it through the mistakes they have made.

Why is this a Secret Key?

Most people do not know that men need more respect and compassion in the relationship. Men are often more insecure then women, they are just better at hiding it. Respect and compassion assure him that you love him and care about him, and that he is good enough for you. If he feels that he is worthy of you, he will become the most devoted person you have ever met. This key unlocks the section in his heart tied to fidelity. If he feels worthy of you, he will do anything to stay there. If he does not feel worthy of you, he will look for someone who makes him feel worthy.

EGO

This all boils down to ego. A man's ego is a powerful thing. Sometimes, if not treated properly, he can become borderline narcissistic. If he feels that he is not getting the respect he deserves, he will look to get it in any way he can. This is where a lot of severe relationship problems stem from. Emotional abuse, physical abuse, infidelity. This is all a problem created when a man is beaten down. Not necessarily by you, but by the world. This is what causes people to split up, and can ruin what seemed to be a perfect relationship.

Men aren't always aware of their ego issues, so they can't tell you what they need. That is not to excuse a man who becomes abusive or a cheater, or even to say that a man is helpless. They know right from wrong, they just don't realize what is causing them to do wrong. If he is abusive or a cheater, then you should leave. No questions asked. Leave. However, if he is just being angry for no reason, maybe you aren't showing each other enough respect and compassion.

How to Show Him Respect

- Be there for him: If he has a gig, or something important, go with him. Even if you aren't interested. Being there for him, and respecting him enough to support him shows him how much you care. If he needs you to listen to him, do so. Let him rant on about something you don't care about, but pay attention. Just because you don't care doesn't give you a free pass to ignore him or tune him out.

- Respect His Privacy: Trust is a big thing in a relationship. Both parties need their privacy on some things, and breaking that privacy is saying that you don't trust your partner enough to give him space. A big thing that a lot of women do is go through his phone. If you can't trust him enough to leave his phone alone, you probably shouldn't be in a relationship. You also shouldn't snoop through his drawers or his personal things. Let him have his privacy, just as you want yours.

- Respect His Personal Space: You don't have to be together every free moment you both have. Sometimes, spending time apart when you have free time is a good thing. You can do your own thing, and don't have to worry about if the other person is having fun. Men need this personal space to unwind after a hard day. Women do as well, but we are focusing on men here. If he doesn't text you back immediately, he is probably in the shower or taking a nice hot bubble bath. It does NOT mean he is cheating on you. Let him have his space without worrying about him stepping out on you. If you trust and respect him, he most likely will not want to do anything to break that trust. But if you don't trust him, he might just give you a reason not to.

- Respect the Fact that He is Human: Men are not robots, and they are not slaves. He has needs, and he needs them tended to at times as well. You cannot expect him to wait on you hand and foot, yet not turn around to do the same for him. Also he will mess up. Don't hang it over his head for the rest of his life. Get through it, and then get over it.

Those are some ways that you can show that you respect him. Men are easy to please, and as they do not have the hormone fluxes that women do, it is more straightforward, but you still have to dig a little to find out his needs. He will give you what you need, if you respect him enough to let him.

Compassion

Compassion is important for when he is having a hard day or makes a mistake. You have to be willing to be compassionate towards someone to ever make a relationship work. Compassion is the difference between healing his heart and breaking it. If you are compassionate, he will trust you with things he doesn't trust anyone else with.

How to Be Compassionate

- Take Care of Him: If he is having a bad day, cook for him. Clean for him. Rub his back and cuddle him. I know this new-age mentality is that women are not a man's slave and that he can do for himself. That may be true, but sometimes you have to take care of him. In return, he will take care of you.

- Be Understanding: Men are human, and they will mess up. Don't overreact if he buys they wrong type of toilet paper, or the wrong grade of milk. They don't always get everything right. You have probably messed up sometimes as well. Did he freak out over the little things?

Relax. If he isn't out killing people, or cheating on you, then discuss it calmly on why you prefer things a different way, and then make like Elsa and 'Let it Go'.

- Don't Ridicule Him: If he is not as advanced as you in some areas, do not make him feel bad for it. If you can read the best, and he can do math the best, combine your strengths. Don't make him feel like less of a person because he can't do what you can. Don't tell him he needs to get better. If he wants to, then help him, but don't tell him he has to.

- Listen to His Problems: The best thing you can ever do is just listen when he wants to talk. Not only will you learn some new things, but you will show him that you are invested in him, and by showing him a little compassion, you make him feel like he is important.

This scenario will show you how respect and compassion can help save a relationship.

Scenario

Rachel was worried about Rick. He had been acting distant lately, and was gone a lot. He always hid his phone and wouldn't let her touch it. Everyone said that he was probably cheating, but she trusted him to have a good reason for all of these things. She didn't want to be let down again by another man.

I will have a talk with him when he gets home tonight. I will ask him why he has been acting this way.

Suddenly she heard a phone ring. She checked her pockets, but it wasn't hers. She investigated the sound, and found her boyfriend's phone behind the toilet. There was a strange number calling.

Should I answer it? No. I trust him. It is probably just a telemarketer, and his phone probably fell behind the toilet this morning, and he didn't grab it cause he was running late to work.

Rachel knew that Rick would be home in a few hours, so she busied herself with errands and cleaning the house up. Five o'clock rolled by, and Rick still wasn't home. She started to get worried, and with no way to contact him, she couldn't allay her fears. But she told herself to remain calm, and that he would show up.

Finally, around seven o'clock, Rick came walking in the door. Rachel flung herself into his arms because she was so worried. Then she noticed that he didn't smell like the fiberglass mill, and he was surprisingly clean for being at work all day.

"Rick. We really need to talk." Rachel whispered, on the verge of tears.

"What's wrong?" Rick asked her

"I have been trusting of you, and I still trust you to tell me what is going on. I am trying not to assume you are cheating. However it is really hard to think of any other explanation why you have been coming home late, hiding your phone behind the toilet and getting strange calls. I didn't answer it by the way. Your clothes are too clean to be coming out of the fiberglass company, and they are the same clothes you walked out of here wearing. You don't smell like you normally do after work. Please just tell me what is going on." Rachel burst into tears.

"Oh Rach." Rick sighed, pulling her into his arms. "I got laid off a couple of weeks ago, and have been looking for a job ever since. That number was probably a job calling so I have to call back tomorrow. I'm late because I have been doing odd jobs to continue making enough money to support us, so you don't have to. I wanted to tell you, I just didn't want you to worry."

"That is what this is all about? You knew I was cheated on several times by my last guy, and you leave me worrying that it is happening again? Babe, I would have understood if you had told me, and I would have supported you, and even got a job myself if need be. I love you, and I want you to tell me about your problems. Please don't hide something like this again."

"Oh Rachel, I love you so much, and I didn't realize how bad it looked. I am so sorry, and I promise to always tell you about these things from now on." Rick said, kissing Rachel passionately.

Discussion

Rachel could have jumped to conclusions and accused Rick of cheating on her, thus making him angry for her not trusting him. However, she decided to ask him about it and listen to what he had to say. She was understanding when he told her what was going on, and let him know she wanted him to bring his troubles to her, even if it meant that he had to put some stress on her. She wanted to take on these problems together.

By being compassionate, and respecting him enough to trust him, she avoided what could have been a really big fight. Instead they were brought closer together, as they opened up with what was bothering them.

Why is this Key Important Again?

You have to respect each other to get anywhere in a relationship. Without respect you have nothing, and you can't truly love someone if you do not respect them. Compassion is needed to ensure that your relationship is not a miserable one. You have to respond with compassion to avoid having an argument blown out of proportion. People are not robots or dolls, they will mess up.

You have to use this key to unlock the part of a man's heart that trusts you. He doesn't open it up for just anyone. Most men do not trust half of the people they say are close to them. They could not be vulnerable to these people. You have to unlock that for yourself.

Chapter 5:
Secret Key #3

Be Confident

Men do not want to be with a woman who is always questioning if she is good enough for him. They want a woman who knows her worth. Men want to know they are with someone who feels valued. If you aren't confident, it makes his job of making you feel secure that much harder. He feels he always has to lift your self esteem, and that can be a hard job for anyone.

Confidence is not always just knowing you are worthy of love, however. It is also taking care of yourself. Taking care of your personal hygiene and keeping yourself groomed. You do not have to be perfect, just put an effort into keeping yourself clean and well kept.

Most people don't realize that this is important in a relationship, and that is what makes it a secret key. It is important to use this to unlock his desires for you if you are looking to start a relationship with him, and you must remain confident and well kept to unlock his never waning desires for you.

Confidence

Everyone has their insecurities, there is no doubt about that. However it is important to not let your insecurities rule your life. You can have some things that make you not so sure about yourself, but you have to be able to work through them.

Confidence is important in any aspect of your life, but it is certainly important in relationships. Not only do you have to be confident in yourself, you have to be confident in your relationship as well. You can't expect a relationship to thrive if you don't have any confidence in it. You have to believe that it will succeed, and that you are good enough for it to succeed.

In this scenario, you will learn more about what poor confidence can do to a relationship.

Scenario

Blake was super insecure. He constantly doubted himself, and if he was good enough for his boyfriend Michael. Michael hated that Blake was so insecure, and wished he could see how gorgeous he was. It caused many fights, because Blake felt that he wasn't good enough and did everything in his power to make Michael see that. Which included picking fights for no reason at all.

I wish I was confident enough to make this relationship work. I am just not good enough for him. He is perfect, and I am a fat lard. I really need to lose weight. I am so fat. Why does he stay with me? Can't he see I'm a disaster?

These are the thoughts that went through Blake's head daily. He couldn't ever get close to Michael, because he was scared that Michael would see that he was a disaster. He constantly had a wall up that Michael was trying to break down.

I'm exhausted. Blake never lets me in, and I'm am so tired of trying to break through the walls he puts up. I wish he could see how much he means to me. He is perfect just the way he is, if only he would stop worrying so much.

Michael was tired of always trying to boost Blake's self esteem, so with a heavy heart, he broke up with Blake.

"I told you I wasn't good enough!" Blake screamed, with tears in his eyes.

"You imbecile! That is the reason I am breaking up with you! You don't feel like you are good enough for me, and I am tired of you ignoring every effort I make to try to show you otherwise! You are perfect just the way you are, and I wish I could have made you see that! I don't want to leave, but I can't keep breaking my heart when you won't let me into yours!" Michael yelled back.

"So you aren't breaking up with me because I'm not breaking up with you, you are merely breaking up with me because I feel like I am not?" Blake whispered

"Yes. I want nothing more than to be with you, but I have to think of my own emotional health as well."

"What if I promised to get help for my insecurities? Would you stay with me? I love you Michael, I just don't want to be hurt anymore. I want you to love me too."

"I do love you Blake, and if you actively get help, then yes, I will stay. But you have two weeks to show me you are trying." Michael said, embracing Blake.

Discussion

Blake's insecurities almost cost him the love of his life. He was so worried about Michael pushing him away, that he didn't realize he was the one doing the pushing. Blake was not confident in himself, and it was tiresome for Michael to always be the one to supply the confidence for the both of them. Michael felt like Blake couldn't truly love him, because he never let him in. It almost destroyed their relationship beyond repair.

If Blake had realized that Michael wanted to be with him for who he was, he would have avoided this whole scene, and been very happy. Let your confidence shine through. You may not feel confident, but fake it until you make it. If you seem confident, you will start to feel confident.

Take Care of Yourself

Men want women to be healthy. This does not mean that you have to eat organic food, and wear full face makeup every day of your life. Just shower regularly, and keep yourself groomed. If you are a slob, and unhygienic, most men will feel that is a sign of lack of confidence, and they will stay away from you. You have to make yourself appear to be ready for a relationship to find the right relationship. If you look like you don't care about yourself you are going to attract someone who doesn't care about you as well.

If you are in a relationship, and start letting yourself go, you will make your man feel like you don't care about the relationship as much as you used to. (This doesn't count if you have kids. Though you should still try to shower regularly) You should always want to keep your hygiene up regardless of your relationship status.

Why is this Key Important?

This key unlocks a man's desire for you. Human's primal instinct is to mate, and men are really close to their primal instincts. He will be looking for a strong woman suitable for carrying his children, so that his offspring are strong and successful. By being confident, and taking care of yourself, you attract men that will value you, and treat you well. If you are not confident, and do not take care of yourself, you often will attract losers and abusers.

Chapter 6:

Secret Key #5

Give and Take on the Lead

This key is one of the most secret keys there are, because most people don't realize that the man doesn't always wear the pants in a relationship. You both have to make the big decisions together, and take turns on the smaller ones. You cannot let one single person take control of the relationship. If you work together, you unlock a bond that allows him to see you as an equal and not as below him.

If you make all of the decisions in the relationship, you allow him to be passive, but if he makes all the decisions, you become passive. Neither one of you should become passive, because this is a one way ticket to a controlling relationship. While it does not always end up that way, fifty six percent of relationships where one person is in charge of most or all of the decisions turn into be abusive relationships.

The solution to avoid this problem is to take turns making decisions. Even the smaller decisions like where to go when you go out to eat, or what to watch on television. On the bigger decisions, make them together. Especially on whether or not to buy a house or start a family, or any big purchase.

Also, take care of finances together, or split them up equally. You cannot give one person complete control of the finances, and expect to not have some control issues. Money is the biggest player in a controlling relationship. If one person has all the control of the money, they can tell the other partner what they can and cannot do, and once you get a taste of that power, it escalates from there.

The best way to avoid this is to get a joint account if you are married that has both of your names on it, so you both can access the funds, or have separate accounts with only your name on it, so the other partner can't access the funds. If you do this though, you have to decide how to split the bills. Otherwise, there will be issues with bills not getting paid, and utilities being shut off. This is if you live together. If not, you don't have to worry about it.

If you don't want to take turns on even the little decisions, then work together to decide everything.

From where you want to eat, to where you want to live. Working together will create a strong bond between you two as well. You will grow closer together as you achieve things together. Think about it. If you make great strides in your life with the one you love, who are you going to celebrate with? That's right, them. So it only makes sense that if you make all your decisions together, you will grow closer due to the fact that you celebrate every achievement as one. You have to want to work together though, otherwise, you will argue more than you work together.

Why is this Key Important?

You want to unlock his heart in a way that makes him see you as an equal rather than a lesser, as society tries to make everyone think. If he sees you as his equal, he will learn to depend on you, rather than walk all over you. There will be less debates on who should make what decisions, and who is always right, because you will both be able to compromise and work together to achieve a blissful relationship.

Relationship Breakthrough

Book 2

CONTENTS

1	Introduction	54
2	Chapter 1: What Do You Want?	56
3	Chapter 2: Secret Key 1 – Open, Honest, Consistent Communication	61
4	Chapter 3: Secret Key 2 – Equality and Respect	73
5	Chapter 4: Secret Key 3 – Acceptance for Who They Are	80
6	Chapter 5: Secret Key 4 – The Pedestal	87
7	Chapter 6: Secret Key 5 – Make Her Smile	91
8	Chapter 7: Special Bonus Tips	94
9	Conclusion	10

INTRODUCTION

Women are a puzzle for men to figure out. Just as women have to figure out men. Each person is a different puzzle and when you find the piece that fits, you have a long lasting relationship. Figuring out the secret to women or the woman you are currently in a relationship with—is easier than ever.

You have a guide that will help you think about the women you are typically interested in dating, currently dating or even married to. Just because you succeed in marrying a woman does not mean the work is over. Marriage is work. Any relationship takes work and involvement.

As a secret key, you cannot expect it to work with every woman you meet. Some women are simply unwilling to open their hearts. You will be given the tools to recognize when a woman is close-hearted, so you know that she is the wrong person for you.

The one thing you cannot forget as you read through this guide—is that you have to decide how much work you are willing to put into the relationship you wish to have. If you are reading this guide hoping you can unlock a woman's heart and then wish to become complacent, your relationship is doomed from the beginning.

Some women also take more work than others. They can have complicated lives or enjoy a little "too much" drama in how they act; therefore, you have to decide what you want in a relationship to gain a serious long term commitment.

You probably didn't think that you are part of the secret key. Yet, you are. Chemistry will only take you so far. A long term relationship, where the woman gives you her full heart begins with you.

So why do you need these "secret keys?" You need them because you want to unlock a woman's heart to its full potential. You want your relationship to go beyond the normal level because you want to be among the 10% who are blissfully happy. Only men who discover the secret of how a woman thinks, what she wants, and her ultimate desire to open her heart to the right man, will be among the elite happy couples in the world.

Discover the path to finally gain access to the "one's" heart that you wish to spend the rest of your life with, through the good and the bad.

CHAPTER 1

WHAT DO YOU WANT?

Do you walk into an electronics store or a car dealership without knowing what you want? No, if you are like most men, you buy magazines that tell you all the technical specs about the latest technology and cars. You also go online to forums and tech websites to do research.

Why would you try to pick up women or try dating sites without knowing what you want? You do not want to do that. If you are like most men, then you have dated, enjoyed one-night stands, and explored the pool of women.

Now, you are reading this book because you are looking for something more. Perhaps, you haven't dated more than a few women and wonder what you are doing wrong?

The men who are successful in relationships, who find those long term marriages—they are the ones who know what they want.

I'll give you an example of a marriage that lasted 42 years. It would have lasted longer if illness did not exist. This couple met when the wife moved into a new apartment complex with two other female friends. The young man, at the time, came up to see if there was anyone he wanted to date or would want to go on dates with him.

He would call up the night he wanted to date and see if someone was willing. He even spent eight months in another state. But, this man realized he had met the one person for him in that apartment.

He came back from living in a different place with one thing in mind—to ensure this woman would date him. He tried his nonchalant style, calling up the day of to ask for a date. She would always refuse because she also had other plans already in the works.

Finally, this man asked, "what do I have to do to get you to go out with me?"

The answer was simple, "call in advance."

The couple dated a few times before Christmas, every week during January and were engaged the day before Valentines.

Life doesn't always happen this way, but you can be sure that the man knew what he wanted. He dated several women, going out when they were available, and enjoying coffee, a meal, or a movie. But, no one caught his attention as much as the woman he married. It took distance to realize that no other woman compared.

If you have not dated very many people, then you need to get out there. You need to start dating more. How else are you supposed to figure out what you want?

I'll give you another example. This couple was together for 17 years and married for 13, almost 14 years. The marriage ended with a divorce and two suffering children. The man dated only two people, marrying the second. The woman had dated more men, but also enjoyed being the center of attention, the person that knows it all, and the person who lies because she doesn't recognize the truth. When the husband asked her father for her hand, the father said, "she is just like her mother, are you sure you know what you are doing?" Her mother constantly spends every dime that is earned, is all about herself, and often depressed and unhappy. Of course, the husband thought he could live with it all, only to find that the woman he was marrying could easily ask for a divorce and immediately move in with another man.

The lesson in this second example is—you can know what you want and what you are capable of living with, but you also have to make allowances for the other person.

A person who cannot love themselves will never be able to love another with their whole heart.

Are you willing to accept being second or loved with less than a whole heart? Are you willing to date or marry someone when, you know, eventually, it will come to an end, it's just a matter of how long it takes?

These are the questions you need to ask yourself as

you begin to learn the secrets to enter a woman's heart completely. Only when you know yourself and what you are willing to accept, can you truly find your way into the right woman's heart.

CHAPTER 2

SECRET KEY #1

Open, Honest, Consistent Communication

Pick up a woman's magazine that has a quiz. I bet that quiz has a section on communication. It probably tests the woman on how communicative her partner is and offers advice on how to elicit more communication. There are millions of these quizzes and articles in magazines, online, and they are all designed for woman by woman. Yet, you can learn something from this concept. Why do you think communication is such a hot topic? It is because women are fundamentally different from men.

Women can be extremely intuitive, even read body language, but women still consider the way men think a mystery. Women cannot believe a man is only thinking about sex. There has to be something more in your brains, right? You are capable of multitasking at your job, of dating multiple women, and holding deep conversations on politics, religion, engineering or something equally complicated—so you must have more on your mind than sex.

You also have feelings. These feelings can be hurt. You can also be excited and feel love. Women are unable to understand why you are unable to talk about these deeper feelings, and demand that you do.

A group of women get together and they catch up. What has happened in your life, what are you doing now, what happened last week. The conversation invariably turns to emotions, but it is not the whole discussion.

Women seek other women for emotional support and understanding because they feel they lack it from the men in their life. Women also work on hormones more so than men.

It's a fact and not something you should fear discussing. A woman can be happy one moment and the wrong words can flip a switch. The grudge can be held for days with the wrong words. A man usually forgets about the issue in a few hours or days, unless the same thing keeps happening.

So, on one hand, women have a need to know your emotions because they cannot understand them unless you tell them. On the other, there are emotional mind fields that you have to navigate as you communicate.

It has been the experience of most women that men do not want to communicate about their feelings. They find it a waste of time. Yet, it is the one thing that will help your woman feel confident in the relationship. It is the way for you to work your way into their heart.

The key is for this communication to be open, honest and consistent.

Defining Open

What does open communication mean? In business, it is a setting where employees are encouraged to share their thoughts and concerns, without the fear of retaliation (reference.com). In a relationship, it is the same thing, only the thoughts and concerns to be shared are about personal situations.

Communication includes issues about one's job, the treatment of the person by their boss, monetary concerns, kids, religion, love, and all other feelings people have.

For example, a family of four sat around a dinner table to discuss whether a move to a new state would be the best option for their family. The discussion included the changes that would occur, the employment options for the parents, and why the move would offer monetary stability versus the current place they lived. Each person was given a chance to discuss their thoughts, fears, concerns, and acceptance of the move.

Another family of four also moved. In this family, the parents sat their children down, said they were moving, and stated where. No communication from the children was allowed as to how they felt or why a move had to occur.

Do you think the children in the first family were more prepared and less unsettled than the second family? Of course, they were. They weighed in with their opinion, fears, concerns, and desires. The second family's children had to keep what they thought to themselves.

Now, consider this example, as a communication between two people: You have two people in a relationship, where one person is always stating what is going to happen, without giving reasons or why it is the best? How unsettled will the partner be? How angry do you think they will become at not having a choice?

Open communication is required to help your woman understand how you think, the reasons behind your actions, and to feel secure in the relationship. If you do not share your thoughts and feelings, how are they to know what you are really thinking? How are they to feel secure that you truly care about them, if they are not kept in the loop or considered part of the equation.

The game telephone provides a good example of this concept. One person starts a statement and by the end of ten or twenty people the statement has changed drastically. By the time your body signals based on your emotions are translated by a woman, they are changed because she is going to interpret them based on how she thinks, just like you try to interpret her behavior based on how you think.

Without communication, you are unable to figure out what each of you is thinking.

Honest Communication

Does this outfit make me look fat? Yes. Ouch. But, it is also how you deliver the answer. You need to be honest because there is one thing a woman does not want—she doesn't want to wear something that does not look good and she will feel embarrassed about later on. Also, here is the kicker—if you lie about how she looks in an outfit—what else could you be lying about?

It is far better to tell the truth when asked for it, then to lie. Furthermore, it is 100% better to speak the truth in any situation. If there is a behavior that bothers you, speak up. One woman told her husband this, "If I start acting like my mother, tell me." She was fearful that she would start displaying certain negative behavior that her mother had and she didn't want to. She was always hurt when being told "you are acting like your mother," but it also helped her realize that a correction to her behavior was required.

A woman who loves herself and gives of herself, completely, to the man she loves is capable of accepting the truth. The anger and stewing for a few hours is better than ignoring the problem or lying to avoid conflict.

Now will all women agree, no. Some women are unable to take the hurt that honest communication provides, but ask yourself, do you want a woman who can give her whole heart because she values your honesty or the woman who keeps a grudge and eventually causes too much pain?

You want the woman who can give her whole heart, so be honest in your communication and explain why you will always tell the truth, even if it is not what the person wants to hear. You'll be valued for this behavior because you are noticing and trying, as well as remaining truthful.

Consistency

More times than I have fingers I have seen relationships start where each person is honest, and communicative. However, after a year or two, the communication stops being consistent. It is like each man and woman believe they have figured the person out and know what they are thinking, so it is less necessary to be communicative.

Wrong.

You cannot become complacent just because it seems like the woman is not demanding communication as often as she was. There are only a few reasons she feels communication is no longer as necessary:

- She thinks she knows you well enough that she can read your moods.
- She is no longer interested.
- She is angry when you don't truly communicate.

If it is the first, then you need to show her that talking each night before you go to sleep is important to you. You need to give of yourself for her to continue giving of herself.

If she is no longer interested, you need to know, so you can move on to find the right person. Sometimes a woman has just as much difficulty breaking off a relationship. She doesn't want to cause hurt when she is unwilling to give her whole heart.

The last reason is fairly easy to discern. If you have not provided any worthwhile communication, then she will turn away, say "fine, whatever," or something along those words and stop trying to communicate with you.

For communication to unlock your woman's heart, you need to:

- Learn to read body language
- Read the subtle nuances in her tone
- And give of yourself before you ask her to give of herself

If you are embarrassed about your thoughts because

they are just about "sex" in that moment—don't be. Tell her. But more than anything, have a time of day when the two of you talk about what happened at work, the challenges or the good things, and plans that you have or things that you want to do.

The conversation does not have to be deep and always about emotions each night. Rather, you are supposed to come together, be honest, be consistent, and just share. You are not to judge, just to listen, with attentiveness. If you only hear the words, then you cannot repeat them.

Here is something else that is usually a complaint from a guy, "all she has ever said are complaints. We never talk about anything other than how much she hates this or that."

Did you ever think that perhaps she is not happy with something that could be changed? Perhaps she needs a new perspective? Maybe, feelings of unhappiness in other areas of her life are making her complain about something else? The biggest one —did you ever think that she only communicates when there is something negative?

Try it, if you are already in a relationship. Track your communication for a week. Did your woman want to talk when she was happy or did she only want to talk when something was bothering her? Did you try to get her to talk about her day or the happy stuff, or did you think "yay, I don't have to try communicating today?"

Your effort to get her to talk when she is happy, will be rewarded. She will know that she can talk about anything, but more that you care to listen about everything. She will learn to talk about the good and the bad, so you don't hear only the unhappy things.

Thus, the ultimate secret is your effort in getting her to communicate about all things, just as much as she is asking you to communicate about anything at all.

One man said, "I didn't think you wanted to listen. I figured it would bore you."

His statement was definitely an insight into why he lacked communication. It was also the key his partner needed to understand that she needed to put more effort into listening.

Most try to say that communication is a two-way street, but is it really? If you drive on a two-way street, you have to keep to your own lane to avoid an accident. I suppose you could "meet in the middle," and block traffic. I'd rather think of communication as a one-way street. One of you has to be illegally driving to meet in the middle, but sometimes that is what it takes for a heart to open. If you are not willing to put in the effort to circumvent any blocks in the way, such as illegally driving down a one-way street, then how can you open up her heart?

She will see the motivation and honesty in your effort to communicate on all subjects that are important to you and her, not just what may be important to her. This will open her heart a little further, and allow her to trust in your feelings for her.

CHAPTER 3

SECRET KEY #2

Equality and Respect

This is a chapter that should be common sense, but more often than not, it is not. Countries were founded on inequality and there are many still struggling with inequality issues to the point that women are killed if they step out of line. Given how sensitive a topic this is—

it should not surprise you that all women want to be treated equally and with respect.

Yes, there are people with more intellect than others, but talking down to them or disrespecting them is not the proper way to communicate. What if you were faced with a woman who had an IQ of 185 and she consistently talked down to you even about simple topics? A man's pride gets pricked pretty easy. It is annoying when a woman is or acts smarter than you. So, why wouldn't it be annoying and insensitive if you are always acting smarter than the woman you are with.

Here is an example: A young man not very well versed in subtle body language and common sense would talk about simple things, a topic that he had in common with a young woman. But, he would often use an arrogant tone with an "I know more than you" attitude. He would tell this young woman things she already knew, like she didn't know the first thing about it.

The relationship didn't last. Nor will any relationship in this situation, when the woman is capable of knowing herself, her own intellect, and a proper way of having a conversation.

It doesn't have to always be about conversation, either. It is just an easy example that helps shore up the previous chapter.

When you communicate in a relationship, the woman wants to be seen as your equal, to have an equal opinion. She doesn't want her words discounted because you know better.

She wants her words to resonate, for you to think about them, and help explain why something else would be better or why her opinion is valued, but not the right approach.

For example, let's say you are married and you have a child. Your child starts to refuse to eat. You might have a different viewpoint than your wife. Your wife might allow the child to go to bed without food until the child finally figures out that starving is not the answer. You might not want your child to go to bed hungry, so you will allow your child to choose a healthy snack such as apples and cheese.

Your wife feels that you are giving in to your child and their refusal to eat healthy things. You might feel that letting your child go hungry, can have unhealthy consequences. Who is right or wrong? That is not the answer. The question is who is going to see results quicker? If the father will get the child to eat healthy foods, then the child will remain healthy. If the child continues to not eat enough, even with healthy snacks then this can hinder the path to a solution. Whereas, starving often gets a child to eat, even a little of something they don't like or a willingness to try it cooked a different way in order to never go to bed hungry again.

The debate won't be answered here because the point is not to solve the question, but to realize that if you refuse to listen to your partner's opinion, harm could be done in more ways than one. You could end up hurting your child and on the other hand, you are putting your wife in a position of disrespect in front of the child.

Dismissing what your partner, whether you are dating, going to the next step, or married, is not going to get her to open her heart to you. Are you always right 100% of the time in all areas? Of course not, and neither is your partner.

The key is for you two to be able to see each other as equals. You look at each other, know your strengths and weaknesses, and compromise when necessary, but never with a disrespectful attitude.

It is okay to point out certain mistakes, but make sure you do it with respect. Value the person and they will open their heart to you. They will also value you more, for showing that you value them.

If you have not yet noticed this is leading to "trust." For a woman to give their entire heart to you—they need to trust you, trust that you understand them, respect them, and value what they have to say or to give in the relationship.

Communication is not the only way to make this known.

Body language is also very important in a woman being seen as an equal. If you ignore something they say or do, it is an act of disrespect, of seeing them as less.

For you it may be complacency. You might be used to the person always cooking your dinner, so you forget to say thank you or take notice of their hard work. The husband or boyfriend who is successful never lets anything go unnoticed.

Car Doors and Other Doors

"She has her own hands; she can open the door."

Have you ever thought this? Perhaps you know someone who has? Maybe, the women you have dated told you it is unnecessary to open doors for her?

Yes, a woman likes to do for herself, but that doesn't mean you should never open a door for her. Choose your moments. Make it a surprise. Even a woman who is capable and willing to open her own doors, appreciates when a gentleman will do it for her. It is based on when you open the door.

For instance, let's say your girlfriend has her arms full of things and there is no hand to open the door. You would immediately open it for her, right? Of course.

The next time you need to open the door is when you are taking her out for a special dinner.

"Let me get the door." This statement tells her that you appreciate that she is coming with you and that she has dressed lovely for the evening. It is a "special" occasion that supersedes the usual rule that she will open her own doors.

If you are running late and it is easier for your partner to open her door, then wait and she doesn't mind opening her own door—it is okay to let her. If she is the type that always needs the door open as a sign of chivalry, then you still, have to open it.

It is not about the door. It is about the effort and respect such an action provides. Again, you let the woman make a choice based on her preferences or you simply ask what she prefers. You choose your moments to be sweet or you always show respect because that is what your heart tells you to do.

There are men who will tell a woman, "I was raised to open doors as a sign of respect. Not complying with this, goes against the respect I have for you."

The key again is to communicate what you know to be right, so that your partner also understands your point of view.

You should back down to show your respect, but also in the same light tell her that you are respecting her more by following through with certain instincts.

Remember these suggestions are examples. You have your upbringing and your partner will have hers. As long as you show mutual respect for each other, and equality of the minds, then you will have a woman who is willing to show you her heart.

CHAPTER 4

SECRET KEY #3

Acceptance for Who They Are

What is the one thing many women have tried to do when they started dating you? They tried to change you. The wrong woman always tries to change her partner. They want you to fit into an ideal they have for a man. There are plenty of reasons for this.

- She is afraid of never finding someone who will accept her

- She feels you are broken and in need of fixing

The two bullet points are the two main reasons she may try to change you. A smart woman will eventually realize that she cannot change the man she is dating. She has to accept him for who he is, his faults and strengths, or find someone else.

You may wish to change the woman you are dating too. Perhaps she doesn't care enough about her appearance? Maybe, she shops and spends too much money? It may be something simple that you do not like, but cannot seem to ignore.

You have an option. You can stop dating a person because she has habits or traits you cannot ignore or you can accept them. It is your choice, but you need to make it.

Don't stay with someone because of your own fear. Yes, men do have fears. There are men out there who fear that they will have to settle for one woman because the one they want is unattainable. Did you ever think that you are not settling, but finding the person who is right for you? Do not settle if things do not feel right and in the same vain do not choose a woman who you cannot accept for her faults and strengths.

If you already have problems or fights due to basic personality clashes, then you are not going to get the woman to stay with you and give her full heart.

The secret is to truly accept, no matter what or to realize that you cannot. If you can accept all of her faults, then you will open her heart a little more, and eventually her whole heart will be yours.

The one thing you cannot do is change your mind

and expect her to open her heart. She has to know that there is consistency within your own heart. You either accept her for who she is or you don't. If you do not really accept her faults, then you will always have doubts in your mind. You will always question or find yourself focusing on the things you cannot accept.

People can only change themselves if they see a problem. They are not going to change because you want the change to happen. For a time, they may try to be better, but after a while, their inherent traits will win out. There is no way around the traits winning, unless the person they are a part of is willing to change.

Yes, you received an example earlier that stated the wife wanted to know when she was acting like her mother. The key here is that she wanted to know. She asked for the truth. She was already in the frame of mind that she may need to change her behavior if she became like her mother.

If you try to point out things to a woman who has not asked or does not think there is something wrong within herself, then you are not going to succeed. She will close her heart and doubt that you can love her fully when you cannot accept all of who she is.

There is also a difference in accepting who a woman is and being her support for the changes that she wishes to make.

What if the woman you are dating had a bad family experience as a child? What if she lacks confidence? Can you deal with her frame of mind and self-doubt? What if you could be her support to help her build her self-confidence without actually pointing out that she needs the help?

It is possible. If you are open and willing to accept the woman for who she is and the potential of who she desires to be, then you are going to find her whole heart is in your hands.

By now you should see a theme in the secrets to a woman's heart: trust and support.

Any woman you date needs to feel they can trust you and that you will be supportive. Without trust and support, she is going to feel like you are only partially in the relationship and she is going to hold back.

It does not matter how many relationships you have had that reach the next level from dating casually to steadily. It does not matter if you have married before and your marriage has failed or is struggling. If you can provide trust and support for the woman you value in your life, you will finally succeed in opening her complete heart to you.

The Pedestal

One man succeeded and another did not. There was a time when one woman was dating two men. She would go out on Fridays with one guy and Saturdays with the other. Both men knew she was dating someone else, but they had never met. One man asked for her hand and was given a "yes." The other took her to a wrestling match the day she received the marriage proposal. The next date he found out she was going to marry the other guy and asked, "are you sure. I love you, you are everything to me, I've put you on a pedestal and don't know how I can live without you being my wife."

The woman's answer: "Your first mistake was putting me on a pedestal."

No one wants to be on a pedestal.

Already it was mentioned that you need to accept the woman for who she is. A part of this discussion is about that very concept. You do need to accept a woman's faults.

More importantly, you cannot raise a woman too higher than she truly is. You cannot have a "celebrity" image of the woman you wish to date.

What if every woman went around trying to find her perfect guy from the romance novels she reads or the songs that have been sung?

You know she won't find this guy because you know men have faults and are not romantic heroes like in the books and movies.

You cannot put a woman on a pedestal and expect a life of happiness to follow.

The minute you put a woman on a pedestal is the minute your relationship is wrong.

You have to be supportive and help her learn to trust you, but you cannot make her a "goddess," in your mind.

Do not keep the rose colored glasses on and reference what you truly want.

What do you wish to see in a woman you can spend your life with? Are you the type of man who needs space, but will never stray? Can you look at attractive women, but know that the one beside you, is the most attractive because of the entire package? If so, then you don't need a pedestal for her. You just need to marry her if you haven't already.

CHAPTER 5

SECRET KEY #4

The Pedestal

One man succeeded and another did not. There was a time when one woman was dating two men. She would go out on Fridays with one guy and Saturdays with the other. Both men knew she was dating someone else, but they had never met. One man asked for her hand and was given a "yes." The other took her to a wrestling match the day she received the marriage proposal. The next date he found out she was going to marry the other guy and asked, "are you sure. I love you, you are everything to me, I've put you on a pedestal and don't know how I can live without you being my wife."

The woman's answer: "Your first mistake was putting me on a pedestal."

No one wants to be on a pedestal.

Already it was mentioned that you need to accept the woman for who she is. A part of this discussion is about that very concept. You do need to accept a woman's faults.

More importantly, you cannot raise a woman too higher than she truly is. You cannot have a "celebrity" image of the woman you wish to date.

What if every woman went around trying to find her perfect guy from the romance novels she reads or the songs that have been sung?

You know she won't find this guy because you know men have faults and are not romantic heroes like in the books and movies.

You cannot put a woman on a pedestal and expect a life of happiness to follow.

The minute you put a woman on a pedestal is the minute your relationship is wrong.

You have to be supportive and help her learn to trust you, but you cannot make her a "goddess," in your mind.

Do not keep the rose colored glasses on and reference what you truly want.

What do you wish to see in a woman you can spend your life with? Are you the type of man who needs space, but will never stray? Can you look at attractive women, but know that the one beside you, is the most attractive because of the entire package? If so, then you don't need a pedestal for her. You just need to marry her if you haven't already.

CHAPTER 6

SECRET KEY #5

Make Her Smile

The key to most women's hearts is to make her smile and laugh. The right woman will accept your personality, whether it is sarcastic humor or witty humor. It is also the effort you provide in making her smile or laugh. For example, a coworker recently knew his female coworker was having a bad day. They are friends and nothing more, as there is a significant difference in age. Yet, the man, going through his own trials, still worked for a good hour to make her laugh and smile rather than to continue crying as she was doing.

This is a man who understands that humor, even in making silly faces, giving out zinger, witty remarks, is the key to making a woman fall a little in love, even if it is only friendship.

You don't have to be the wittiest. You may have a stupid joke that makes one groan more than laugh or smile. However, the effort in trying to make the woman smile, to make her laugh, will instantly make her heart melt.

Gifts are Important

Surprise gifts are important to a woman. They consider these gifts as supportive or endearing because you are paying attention to her. There are times when life gets routine, mundane, and even filled with complacency on both of your sides. The trick is to come home with a surprise.

Flowers are nice for some women. For others, they are an instant allergy issue. Some men feel that flowers are going to die, so why spend the money, when something else can be provided, such as a vacation from saving money on the little things.

The key is to know what your woman believes and what you can do that will matter to her heart. Sometimes it can be the silliest thing or the simplest. What if you both love tattoos? Did you ever think about getting a tattoo of a symbol or date that matters to both of you?

Perhaps, it is as simple as coming home with a card. Maybe when she goes on a business trip you hide a card in her bag moments before you say goodbye at the airport.

Gifts do not have to be expensive, they do not have to be jewelry, but they do need to be thought of and given. Yes, some women prefer expensive gifts, even demand them, and if you have a wife or partner like this, then you need to comply sometimes. It goes back to accepting and knowing the woman you have in your life. However, it doesn't mean that small things like cards and spontaneous gifts that are not expensive won't move her heart.

It is all about what you know about her desires, what she is used to, and what will make her smile and love you because of the effort you have shown. You can also show a woman used to expensive gifts that it is not the money, but the honesty behind the gift that matters the most.

CHAPTER 7

Special Bonus Tips

Not all women will fit your personality. There are some women who should not be in relationships or marry, unless they can find a partner who is just like them in the key ways. There are even some women who will never open their heart and find true happiness because they cannot find it in themselves. These bonus tips will help you look at relationships and women, so you might succeed, when you have faced certain issues such as being in a bad relationship, failing to be supportive in small ways, or even noticing her each and every day.

Things to Look Out For

- Does your current partner feel love is shown through how much you buy her?

- Does she flirt with other men to see if you are getting angry or noticing what she is doing?

- Does she seem to pick a fight or get angry for no reason you can see?

- Has she started to withdraw from you?

- Is she starting to ignore you, your phone calls, or breaking dates?

These are a few signs that you need to look out for in understanding that she is not the woman for you. Some of these can also be a sign that she may have a psychological issue that she cannot get passed and will eventually affect the relationship.

For instance, have you ever date a woman who lies, who tries to separate you from friends and family, needs "things" to feel you love her, and is always thinking about herself? This can be the sign of a narcissist. A narcissist is someone who views themselves as the most important, cannot handle when someone else is more important, is often arrogant, and knows everything. This same person also blames everyone around them for being at fault and for doing things they are actually doing.

Toxic relationships like this need to be avoided, even if you feel you can live with this person's faults. Drama is another word that has been applied to women who seem to cause conflict, always pick a fight, and have a healthy sexual appetite that never seems satisfied with just one person.

Only you can truly say what type of relationship you are looking for, but there are definitely signs that you need to watch out for with regards to women and drama they can create.

- A woman can call you several times a day or demand that you call them often.

- They may ask where you were and not trust your answer.

- They may text or try to start up a conversation that is too deep on the first meeting.

- They may complain and find nothing happy.

These are just a few other signs that a woman may not be right for you or perhaps anyone. Someone who is obsessive without actually dating you can have psychological issues that require a professional. It may not be nice to say of one's own sex, but it is also the truth. Some women need to recognize their failings and accept those in order to find a healthy relationship, otherwise they are "crazy" in their actions towards men, bordering on obsessive.

Signs of a Wrong Relationship

Relationships do not have to be filled with "crazy" or drama to be wrong for you. There are definite signs that a woman is not right for you, when she is unwilling to give her heart to you. It is not a matter of you trying harder to be supportive, and not complacent in the relationship.

Here is an example of a woman. See if you can see why she might be wrong for a relationship with you.

- She prefers her own company to others.
- She has social anxiety.
- She needs a routine and does not like that routine to be interrupted.
- She is hyper-organized, hating when someone fills up a space she just cleaned.
- She cannot trust easily.

- She is unwilling to be hurt and face the loss of a husband, preferring to die before any of her family, so she doesn't have to face that horrible situation.

- She also has a dislike of touch, something no one can pinpoint a cause for, but one that holds her from a deep physical relationship.

Obviously, this is an extreme example, but take note of it. Sometimes the signs are subtle and other times there is a big sign saying "this is not right." A woman who does not allow physical contact after three dates either has issues with physical contact or does not see you as a sexual partner. A relationship that is not right for you will have fights, ups and downs, and disagreements on the main issues. You won't be able to agree on politics, religion, children, and life in general.

Additional Effort Options

A couple was having trouble in their marriage. The wife was unhappy. The man knew it, but couldn't figure out what to do. He decided he would ask her each morning, "what can I do to make your day better?" At first, his wife thought he was being insensitive and joking. After he kept asking she realized that he meant it and started answering, as well as asking how she could make his day better.

Such a simple phrase and the care behind it saved the marriage. You can do something like this in your relationship. It doesn't have to be a big deal. It can be something as simple as asking how your partner's day was or how you can make it better.

It can also be something that will make her smile. The married couple of 42 years is another great example. One child was grown, married, and nearing having children. The second child left home to live 3,000 miles away. Living as just the two of them, the wife was missing her children. To make her day better, the husband took one of the stuffed animals his daughter left when she moved away, and started creating funny scenes.

One day the orangutan stuffed animal was holding a fake cigarette and reading in their bed. The next day it was playing chess with one of the wife's stuffed bears of similar size. For over a week, the husband would wake up, create a scene, leave for work, and his wife would come home to it. She would smile. Now she has pictures of these scenes to help her memory, since the husband passed away from early onset dementia.

These little efforts changed the wife's outlook for the day, the ache in her heart from missing her daughter, and now is a comfort to her with him gone.

What can you think to do that would have such a lasting impact because it is guaranteed to open the woman's heart for life.

Flowers are acceptable, of course, and even desired by most women. But, if you have the imagination, find something that can truly make her smile, laugh, or even cry with happiness. It matters.

Helping Your Partner become a Better Her

The couple who spent 42 years together respected each other, loved each other, and were best friends as well as husband and wife. One of the biggest impacts the husband had on his wife, was mutual respect, equality, and the power to give her what made her a better version of herself. This is not about changing the person, but giving her the tools to go after what she desires.

The wife was told by her mother on more than one occasion that she was stupid, worthless and that her mother wished she had never been born. Her only choice of work was to go to a trade school. Given the year she graduated, her only real choice was to become a hairdresser. It was not something she hated, but her husband also gave her the choice of being able to do more and spend more time with her children as they grew.

In fact, she started working with her husband on construction sites building houses as a family. It gave her more freedom to spend with her children, as well as spend every day with her husband. When she would ask can "I do this or do that," such as take ballet, he told her "you never have to ask. You can do what you want to do."

He gave her the power to try different things and be who she was, without judgement. It helped that they had the money for her to try new things, but all the same he told her they were equal that the money they made was hers to spend as she wished.

Now, she was also brought up in a poor family, so

spending money was a difficult decision. She never spent money that was earmarked for bills, groceries, and necessary monthly expenses. She was responsible in the spending, but also given the chance to explore and do.

It made her heart open more for this husband. You may find that you are drawn to such a woman yourself. You also need to realize that while she is becoming a better version of herself because of you, she can also make you a better version of yourself. It is not about changing who you are inherently, but about taking what you are, loving who you are, and helping you be the best you can be even in the face of adversity.

The person who can allow this and accept such help in return is the person that can form a long term, lasting relationship with the right woman. It is also the person who will have the whole heart of the woman he loves.

Withholding Due to Fear

A lack of support and trust in a relationship can lead to the woman you are dating or married to, fearing to give her whole heart to you. There are subtle signs you need to look for if the woman fears giving her heart.

- She will withhold herself too.
- She will often go on trips without you for business or to visit family, and not call.
- She will test to see if she can live without you.
- She will test you in communication to be more open in conversation.
- She will become angry or distant if you answer wrong or continue to withhold.
- More fights will occur.

- She will start to ask where you see the relationship going.

These are fear tests that she is giving you. She is hoping that you will realize her fear and start to open up, start to pay attention, and show her through action not words, how much she means to you.

If she is not the right woman, then don't let her live in fear. If she is the woman you wish to gain her whole heart, recognize the fear, address it, and start changing how you communicate, offer her your trust, and support.

What do you do if a woman says she is moving out? Do you let her or do you ask her what is going on?

If you have established open communication, where she feels she can trust you, but is not receiving proper support or respect, she will tell you her fear. If you have done nothing to gain her trust, respect, support, or communication she will be evasive and tell you "it's just not working or it's me not you."

For the right woman, you will strive to correct yourself to make her more comfortable and recognize your fault and the fear of the relationship she is feeling. If you cannot give her that, then you need to allow the relationship to end, learn from it, and start looking for the woman who is right for you.

Are you Clinging

There are certain turn offs for a woman.

- She does not want to be your mother.

- She does not want to constantly clean up after you.

- She does not want to cook you every meal you eat.

- She wants you to make an effort.

- She does not want you to call 10 times a day.

- She wants you to respect what she says and remember what she says.

- If she tells you no, then it is no. Not maybe, not flirting, not suggestive.

- If she asks for your opinion or a decision on what you want to do—give her one.

- A woman wants a decisive man, who knows himself, and is not afraid to laugh at himself.

Above all she does not want a man who clings. She does not want someone who is obtuse to her feelings or the subtle information she is giving him. She wants someone who is willing to pay attention, to be supportive, who will try to gain her trust, and love her so she can open her heart to him.

CONCLUSION

The secret to breakthrough with women are simple — create a situation where you are supportive and gain her trust. To be the one, you have to give of yourself before you ask her to give you all of herself.

Each woman is different in personality, tastes, and needs, but they are also fundamentally the same in needing to be important, respected, equal in mind and body, and loved unconditionally.

Only when you can be yourself, honest, supportive, and respect her fully can you be "the one" for her.

You also have to realize that sometimes a woman is unwilling to open her heart. Sometimes she may not see you as the one or no matter what you do to try opening her heart, she simply cannot.

If you can recognize that she is never going to open her heart to you, then you can move on to a woman who is willing.

Sometimes you definitely get lucky and met the "one" for you and marry three months later. Sometimes it takes years. You have to be open. You have to be willing. You cannot be complacent. You also have to know what you are looking for to recognize her when she comes along.

If you don't know your own mind, then you won't be able to see the woman who is right for you. She could be next to you, waiting for you to see her and waiting to open her heart to you. She may be the next woman you meet through an online dating service.

Only when you have the secret key to making sure you are supportive and giving her a reason to trust you—will you succeed.

You can do this. You now have insight into a woman's mind, examples of success and non-success. Now, take what you have learned and apply it to you and your unique situation or woman.

Thank you!

And I wish you all the best in your journey to be the best you can be with your loving partner!

J.

CPSIA information can be obtained
at www.ICGtesting.com
Printed in the USA
LVHW080451211120
672131LV00006B/397